The
Complete Mother
by
Phyllis Diller

The Complete Mother

by

Phyllis Diller

Illustrated by Iwao Takamoto

DOUBLEDAY AND COMPANY, INC.
GARDEN CITY, NEW YORK

9557

Publishing Consultant: J. P. Tarcher, Inc.

CONTENTS

FROM HERE TO MATERNITY

This book was written by a practicing mother. Just like prisoners who keep their spirits going up with the thought they will write a book about it later, I bore this in mind while raising my children.

I've noticed when I see kids playing house today that fewer and fewer are crying, "I want to be the mother!" In order to stop this trend, I want to give mothers some helpful suggestions. I fully understand that there will be days when you will think that the only good thing about having a family is that when you're at a dinner party and someone asks, "Do you have children?" you can say, "Yes." However, there's much to be grateful for. Always remember, the way things are in the world today, if you goof up being a mother, your mistakes aren't going to be as noticeable.

Try to give the impression that you enjoy being a mother. No matter how your children are misbehaving in the morning, never run after your husband in your bathrobe screaming, "Take me with you!" and if someone calls your husband after 8:00 don't say, "I'm sorry, but he's already escaped to the office."

Keep in mind the fact that if someone saves your kid's life, it doesn't look good to give a reward of less than 25 cents, and whatever you do, don't store your child's winter jacket in the attic while he's wearing it.

1.

YOU'RE NOBODY
'TIL SOMEBODY LOVES YOU
AND THE NEXT THING
YOU KNOW,
YOU'RE A DEN MOTHER

The Spacing Program

It would seem that something which means poverty, disorder and violence every single day should be avoided entirely, but the desire to beget children is a natural urge. Couples usually try to combine judgment with that instinct and this is known as Family Planning. However, Nature does not always seem to be on our side, and we are often taken unawares.

An unexpected pregnancy is like being on a hijacked airplane. Therefore, even though it may not do any good, it can't do any harm to tell your husband your feelings about not wanting to get pregnant. Don't say, "Let's vote on it by secret ballot."

Fang and I believed in planned parenthood. We

didn't have any children until after we were married. I always told my friends, "This baby was planned." However, I found nobody believed me because I'd always say it while crying.

And even when you are planning children, you can't plan how they will turn out. Mine always seemed as if I'd picked them up in a bar.

In all those years and through all those pregnancies I did pick up a little wisdom.

1. Children are improperly spaced if you have a baptism and a wedding in the same year.

2. Bear in mind that popsicles, ice cream bars and other treats come in cartons of six, so don't have an extra child that will force you to break into another carton.

3. You've already had too many children if there isn't room on the outdoor grill for one hamburger apiece.

4. Stop having children before it becomes necessary for you to have them wear name tags.

I'm A Planned Parenthood Dropout

In spite of all my good intentions, I was the "Believe It or Not" of the Maternity Ward. I had quintuplets the hard way—one at a time. That's a lot of pickles and ice cream. After I had five kids in a row, Fang nicknamed me Bingo.

1. I really never minded being fertile—but I have to admit there were times when I considered crop rotation.

2. My neighbor asked me: "Are you expecting!" I said: "I'm not expecting. I'm sure!"

3. I had so many kids I had dealer's plates on my baby carriages.

4. At one time our bedroom looked like a Used Crib lot.

5. One day I picked up a bag of flour out of a shopping cart and burped it.

6. Once I even said to Fang, "I'll bet you don't even know how many kids we got" and he answered, "Well, when I used to count them it made me nervous."

7. I always say, "You show me a woman with 15 children and I'll show you an overbearing woman."

Oh, how I wish I could find the smart aleck who wrote in my high school year book—"May all your troubles be little ones."

There Is Not Always Room For One More
Or
Have You Ever Noticed That Most Of The People Who Favor Birth Control Have Already Been Born?

When Fang and I got married he said, "In a couple of years we will hear the pitter patter of little footsteps." So I set traps. Nevertheless, I had chronic pregnancy, which is not surprising since even as a child I was accident prone. With me, birth control meant not having the kid until I got to the hospital. I was pregnant so often I felt like the bag on the vacuum cleaner. But you don't have to have so many children. There are three great methods of birth control. They are:

1. Thinking about what other people will say if you get pregnant again.

2. A garlic salami before retiring.

3. The pill.

Eleven million women in the world use birth control pills. They are called progressive. One billion

women don't use birth control pills. They are called "Mama."

Of course, there are older types of contraceptives than the pill, but as of this writing, no one has figured out how to knit anything that works.

Doctors recommend birth control pills be taken the same time each day. Select the time of day when your children are at their worst—then it's easier to remember to take your pill.

If your children come across your birth control pills and ask about them, an honest answer you can give is, "I take them to prevent a nervous breakdown." Always remember—they are not sold with a money back guarantee.

In the future, birth control methods will be entirely different. By the year 2000 we'll be growing babies from laboratory cultures. Imagine turning down the lights, putting soft music on the record player, mixing a couple of martinis, and then being told by a test tube, it's not in the mood.

"All In Favor Say, 'Aye'—All Opposed, Say, 'Goodnight'"

Some people are very relaxed and calm in the face of great danger. In this category are women who use the Rhythm Method. This kind of woman would be absolutely cool facing a firing squad. If you use the Rhythm Method, keep these facts in mind.

1. It should be agreeable to both parties. You are dealing with the husband you love. You cannot do things like shout, "Yankee go home!" On the other hand, the man should be co-operative. Only a very immature husband upon refusal will threaten to hold his breath or call his mother.

2. It doesn't help to have a written contract.

3. No matter how short the fertility period is—it's long enough.

4. Fertility forecasting is almost as accurate as weather forecasting.

5. If you plan on using the Rhythm Method it helps to be on your toes—on your toes cleaning shelves or on your toes washing windows until your husband falls asleep.

After 5 years of the Rhythm System, Fang and I decided 5 kids are enough. But you can say this for it . . . the Rhythm Method has produced some very beautiful families.

Lowering The Bloating Age

The trend today is for girls to get married and have babies very young. Perhaps they feel that before they forget it they should put to use what they learned in their Hygiene class. You will know you are too young to have a baby if:

1. You call your Girl Scout leader from the hospital to see if you can get a merit badge for childbearing.

2. Your mother's reaction to your pregnancy is to make you go sit in the corner.

3. You demand orange flavored, chewable calcium pills.

4. You tell your friends, "I'll have it in the second semester."

One kid in our neighborhood rushed his new wife to the hospital thinking she was pregnant because she cried all the time. The doctor examined her and said, "She'll be O.K. in a few days; she's just teething."

The Menopause That Refreshes—But Not Always

One of my kids was telling a neighbor: "My mama is 43 years old and she's going to have a baby." My neighbor said: "I'm not going to stand here and listen to horror stories." Of course, some people consider a baby in middle age to be a dividend, a wonderful blessing that will some day be the greatest consolation of old age. These are people trying to console a pregnant middle-aged woman. You must continue being careful. You will know that you are too old to have a baby:

1. If you are ten years beyond the age that you would be permitted to adopt.
2. If you call your doctor to find out if Geritol adds to morning sickness.
3. If you are the first woman in history to have her maternity costs paid for by Medicare.

If you become pregnant late in life you can take consolation from the fact that a pregnant woman over 40 is not expected to be a good sport.

A woman this age who discovers she's pregnant shouldn't feel it's unnatural for her to have the urge to shoot herself—or for her husband to have the urge to load her gun.

Your Obstetrician Never Had A Baby

Once one of my kids said to a neighbor's child, "Let's play pregnant." The other kid said: "O.K.! What do I do?" and my kid replied, "You faint and I'll throw up."

Very few women get pregnant for the sheer love of nausea, but morning sickness *is* part of the basic pre-natal condition. It can begin any time after the end of the late movie and often lasts all day. After three months of this, it's a thrill just to leave the room walking.

It always makes a woman feel smart when she thinks of buying ordinary styles three sizes larger than she usually wears. You can buy several of these and you'll be able to wear them at least a week or ten days.

I gained so much weight when I had my last baby, I looked like a Cadillac pushing a Volkswagen. When they wheeled me into the Delivery Room, the cart got a flat tire.

There are a number of things you should remember about your condition:

1. Early detection means nothing.

2. A silver knife does not keep down the swelling.

3. By far the most common craving of pregnant women is not to be pregnant.

4. Tranquilizers work only if you follow the advice on the bottle. It says, "Keep away from Children."

Show And Tell

You've settled down to wait for your baby. Well, at least the house is clean because of all the ceilings you've scrubbed and walls you've painted in the hope of discovering you weren't really pregnant.

1. Don't make excuses for being pregnant. It sounds silly to explain your condition by saying, "I'm just one of those people who can't turn down anything free."

2. Even if you are eager to show your condition, it's not a good idea to starch your maternity dress.

3. Getting into the spirit of motherhood may take getting into the spirits. Give yourself pep talks—at least every ten minutes.

4. I was about 3 months pregnant and my neighbor asked me bluntly: "Are you going to have another baby?" "Heavens no!" I said, "I'm just carrying it for a friend."

5. Be careful not to let the whole world know you're expecting as soon as you find out yourself. It will make nine months seem like nine years. Your maternity dresses will seem like *E*ternity dresses.

In fact, don't tell anyone until it's absolutely necessary—especially your husband.

That's The Glory Of Love
Or
How To Tell Your Husband

The 5 times I told Fang I was pregnant went like this:

1. I played a record of "Rockabye Baby" and he kissed me.

2. I said coyly: "The baby is going to have a playmate!" He said: "You bought a dog?"

3. I said: "Hey there! That silly stork is landing here again." We shook hands.

4. I said: "Guess what!" He shrugged his shoulders.

5. On the day I whispered to Fang, "We're going to have a fifth," he said: "Great! I'll get the ice and the mix."

I know you will want a novel way to tell your husband he is to become a father. Here are a few suggestions:

1. Write on the bathroom wall, "Margaret Sanger is a rat fink."

2. Say, "Is there room in your billfold for one more picture?"

3. "Honey, how would you like to get a little more value out of our babysitting money?"

4. "How would you like to see Father's Day work into something really big for you?"

5. "Don't you think it's too bad to put forth all that effort of setting a good example just for BILLY?"

6. "Would you like to meet somebody new?"

The First Half Hour Flies

Since you already have proof positive that idle hands make mischief, the following list will help you while away the 6,576 hours of your pregnancy. But who's counting? 6,575 . . . 6,574 . . . 6,573 . . .

1. Don't talk to anyone who describes labor pains as anything more than uncomfortable.

2. There is much talk about a husband feeling rejected after the baby comes. To eliminate this danger, start rejecting him *before* the baby comes.

3. If you have an intercom in your home, have it disconnected. Why make sure you hear every squawk from the nursery when there's a chance you might be able to sleep through some.

4. Beware of pre-natal influences. I have a friend who had quintuplets after going to the movies to see Birth of a Nation.

5. Take a tour of mental institutions and have one selected. You will not have an opportunity to do this after your breakdown comes.

6. Go to pre-natal classes at the hospital. You will learn a lot from these. The speaker is a phony if he ends his talk with, "Remember, the baby will only make your life more interesting."

7. Above all, get out and go places while you are awaiting the birth of your baby. Your maternity dress is the cheapest babysitter you'll ever have!

The Gift That Keeps On Taking
Or
From Stretch Marks To A Stretched Budget

Who ever coined the phrase "free love" has obviously never supported a family. Just because you have a big family it's not necessarily economy size.

How much does it cost to have a baby? You might as well ask, "How high is up?" In fact, that's a better question because people don't have babies after they ask it.

Every obstetrician would have to use smelling salts if he told a mother-to-be on her first visit what will be the total cost of raising this child. His motto should be "send no money now – You'll be billed later."

Once when I explained the facts of life to my kids, they wanted to know the name of the bird with the big bill that brings babies. I said: "The bird with the big bill is the doctor." The expenses start immediately.

1. Lights on all night because you can't sleep once you've found out you're pregnant.

2. Long distance telephone calls to Mother.

3. Maps (looking for a way "out").

No matter how optimistic you are, you certainly must realize it is impossible to save enough green

stamps in nine months to get the buggy, the high chair, crib, mattress, bathinette, sterilizer, vaporizer, stroller *and* playpen.

When you finally figure out how much more your husband will have to earn, pin a slip with the total on it to a bouquet of flowers and do not, under any circumstances give it to him until he has had 2 martinis, is slightly aglow and feeling extremely secure. Then make sure you're out of the house when he sobers up and turns blue.

What Not To Name The Baby

Be very careful to select a name your child will be happy about. There are lots of Bobs and Bills but only one Samovar.

We named all ours . . . "Kid." Of course, they have different first names — "stupid kid" — "ugly kid" — "clumsy kid." We've got so many kids, I've run out of names — to call my husband.

1. Make the name simple, not like our neighbor's child, Bartholomew, who was held back in first grade because he couldn't spell his name.

2. Give your son a common name—one that when it is yelled out by the teacher it isn't quite so definitely established who it is.

3. Give your daughter an unbelievably homely name so that young men chase her because they think she's named for someone who is going to leave her money.

4. Girls are particularly sensitive. I know one young girl who keeps begging her mother to divorce her father and marry another man just because her first and last name go together so badly.

If your last name is		don't call her
1.	Belt	Chastity
2.	Pad	Lily
3.	Bopper	Teenie
4.	String	Gee
5.	Carr	Kitty
6.	Hind	Bea
7.	Keene	Peachie
8.	Cohen	Vanella
9.	Pitt	Olive
10.	O'Graph	Mimi

If your last name is		don't call him
1.	Vale	Noah
2.	DeBumper	Ben
3.	Heeler	Ward
4.	Furter	Frank
5.	Handler	Mann
6.	Labor	Manual
7.	Waggon	Chuck
8.	Walk	Jay
9.	Horn	Otto
10.	Quido	Amos

Our neighbor has unusual names for her children. There was Vamp, Drack, Jeckyl, Hyde and Frank. I thought she made a mistake with Frank, but the kid said it was only a nickname, short for Frankenstein.

Son Worshipers

Usually everyone wants a boy but it is unwise to set your heart on any particular sex. It is rather pathetic to see a little girl named Gregorita or Rodney Ann.

1. Be sure not to make any rash commitment to give your husband a son. Attempts to carry out this pledge can become pretty monotonous (or however you want to describe it).

2. If you have a son after 8 or 9 daughters—don't be so overjoyed you just name him "boy."

3. It's nice to have both sexes represented, but, if you do have all boys or all girls, just say, "I decided to specialize."

These Are A Few Of My Least Favorite Things

Since it is very easy to get a persecution complex in the Delivery Room, you should approach it with Pollyanna thinking—like having a baby can make you forget about a sore throat. Have enough rapport established with your obstetrician so that, when

you're having the baby, any request you make will not just be thought of as an attention-getting device. As they wheeled me in I kept telling them, "Can't you read—that door says 'No Admittance!' "

The Delivery Room situation is the exact opposite of putting your best foot forward. You will never be so brightly lit, so completely the center of attention and at your very worst. Just at the time when you would like to crawl into a dark hole and call the whole thing off the whole world is lit up like a super-market opening and YOU ARE IT!!

My persecution complex started during one delivery when I was a little slow with the push-push and the doctor and nurses became bored. They took out a deck of cards and played rummy on my stomach while waiting for me to get with it.

To make your life almost tolerable, here are some tips:

1. Find out who the interns are. During the delivery of one child, I was pleading for a hypo from a fellow in a white uniform that was there to fill the pop machine.

2. Tell everyone the book you are planning to write is about hospital personnel.

3. If they ask if it's all right to take a coffee break, say, "NO."

4. Close your eyes if you notice that the doctor is wearing a rabbit's foot!

Some women think it is important to be awake during the birth of their baby. This is ridiculous. It may be the last sleep you get for months!

Every so often an expectant mother is asked if she minds having a class of student nurses observe the birth. I was very gracious when this request was once made of me, but later on I got just a little upset.

1. One of them said, "I didn't get that. Would you mind doing it again?"

2. Another was a former salesgirl from Sears. She hadn't quite made the transition. As I was leaving the hospital she asked: "Do you want the baby in a bag, or would you like it gift wrapped?" For a tiny moment—I had a glimmer of hope—I thought maybe I could give it away.

Many hospitals have a program called "lying-in" where the baby stays in the room with the mother. This naturally isn't for me. I fight being a live-in mother at home.

What A Cute Little Monkey . . .
An Ugly Baby, But A Cute Monkey

Even though he looks like he was delivered by an anthropologist instead of an obstetrician, be prepared to love your baby, no matter what. It is impossible to get them custom made. His skin will be shriveled and wrinkled. In fact, he will look like something that's been machine washed that should have been hand-laundered. While in the hospital it's normal to hope from feeding to feeding that the nurse will suddenly come in with a beautiful baby, announcing the ugly one was just a case of mistaken identity.

Children should be seen and not heard, and new babies shouldn't even be seen!

1. One mother I knew refused anaesthetic during the delivery and then screamed, "Ether! Ether!" when they held the baby up for her to see.

2. When the nurse hands you your baby and you look at him for the first time, immediately say, "Isn't he beautiful!" *NOT* "What kind of a joke is this?"

3. The one advantage you get from an ugly baby is that you can always say to the obstetrician: "You mean you're charging full price for a baby that looks like that?"

If your baby is exceptionally homely, while walking him wear a nurse's uniform. Only once did this technique backfire for me. A nasty old bat approached my baby carriage, leaned over and really let me have it. She said: "I have never seen such an ugly baby in my life. Just look at those red blotches. It looks like it has mange. And those eyes. They're speckled. How can a 6 month old baby have blood-shot eyes on milk? And that one tooth, right in the middle. I wonder what's going to happen when the rest start coming in. And there is a nose that looks like something a kid would build at the beach with sand . . ." I said: "I'm the Mother." Then she looked up at me and fainted.

He Must Be Good For Something But I Just Can't Figure Out What

Do not expect any help from the father. When I told Fang it was time to go to the hospital with the first baby, he got hysterical. He said: "This is my bowling night!" We finally reached an agreement. He agreed to carry my suit case out to the car and I carried his bowling ball.

When he called the hospital to report that I was in labor, the nurse, trying to calm Fang down said: "Is this her first baby?" He said: "No, this is her husband."

Going to the hospital, I drove while he sat in the back seat fanning himself with my insurance policy. When he filled out the admittance form, under Name of Parents he wrote, "Mom and Dad."

When I was in the hospital Fang took our kids to the doctor every week for a check-up. Later I found out he was selling their blood. He also insisted that my confinement was a separate vacation and demanded equal time for hunting or fishing.

The day we left the hospital Fang loaded the car with flowers and gifts. We nearly made our escape but some idiot nurse came screaming, "You forgot the baby!" Of course Fang had an excuse. Somebody had told him the baby wasn't his. It was the doctor. We hadn't paid his bill.

Out Of The Mouths Of Babes Comes Drooling

Nobody likes feeding a baby, least of all the baby, so have him on a good schedule. Give him a bottle during four of your favorite TV shows.

1. Check cereals to see which one provides the greatest amount of pep and energy, and make sure you never buy it.

2. Make a deal with the milkman. He'll take the six o'clock feeding if you buy some cottage cheese.

3. Always have plenty of formula ready. A tiny baby doesn't understand when you say, "Dinner will be a little late."

4. Not one baby in 20 will recognize the taste of vodka in his formula.

5. Our kids broke so many bottles I finally gave up. I just gave them formula popsicles.

6. I'll never forget the wonderful day our kid went off the formula and started eating solids—crayons, erasers, doorstops . . .

Sometimes after a meal your baby will cry. Burping may be the solution. However, when burping a baby do not use too strong a motion, out of respect to the clothes you are wearing. I once hit a kid on the back so hard we had to do over a whole wall!

What To Do During The Two O'Clock Feeding

Never wake up your baby for the 2 o'clock feeding. He may *always* cling to the idea you aren't all there.

The only person you can possibly consider calling at that hour is your hospital roommate. You should have a few things to pass the time at this bleak hour.

1. See how many words you can make out of your baby's name.

2. Count the number of commercials during the feeding and then work on cutting them down during the next feeding.

3. Think of arguments to present on why you need a new outfit, why you need a cleaning lady, or why you need a car of your own. However, no matter how great they are, don't wake your husband up at 2:00 to present them. Chisel them on a stone tablet and hit him over the head with them in the morning.

4. Look around for smudges and cobwebs that you didn't notice during the day and write down their location to catch them next month when you clean.

The Night Has A Thousand Cries... Unfortunately So Does The Day!

"Give your baby a lot of attention" is an unnecessary piece of advice that experts are constantly giving. Babies will have it no other way.

Some babies cry all night. This is known as colic. The only advantage of a baby having colic is that

you do not have to keep checking to see if he is breathing.

Don't worry about not waking up for the 2 o'clock feeding when your baby is hungry. At that time babies always sound like they're crying over a PA system. There are some ways to stop a baby from crying.

1. Threaten to cut him out of your will.

2. Stand over the crib yelling, "You're a cry baby, you're a cry baby!"

3. Tell him he's making too much noise and the days of the big bands are over.

4. Tell him he's a disgrace to his nappy suit.

Babies need a lot of sleep and so do parents—need a lot of baby's sleep.

That Certainly Is Some Baby

New babies get very high viewing ratings. No matter how it seems, people are not being malicious in coming to visit you the first day you're home from the hospital.

1. It's not polite to post visiting hours on the front door.

2. If your child cries everytime your mother-in-law comes near her, don't say, "Now isn't that funny? —if you were a dog or a cat, she wouldn't be a bit afraid."

3. When a caller is polite enough to ask to hold your baby, take it back after a reasonable length of time. Don't make him feel he must take it home with him.

4. Don't feel bad if your baby isn't pretty and people say unkind things. My mother survived and these were some of the tactless remarks she heard when people viewed me in the buggy:

"If I were you, I wouldn't wipe the pablum off her face."

"Cheer up. If there are ten more babies that are born looking like that, I'm sure someone will start a drive."

"When she reaches adolescence, you can probably have her face capped."

Sis, Boom-Boom, Bah!

Right before your very eyes these bundles from heaven become bundles of laundry. Diapers soon get to be a drag, so the mother tries potty training as soon as possible. This is the most painful part of child training. Of course, I had so many kids, if they wanted to be changed they had to take a number. I've stuck so many diaper pins in my skin when I take a drink I leak.

1. Trying to catch him is the object of the project. This gets very discouraging. You can hang around a kid eight hours and the minute you leave it happens.

2. Educate yourself to recognize the "look" on your baby's face. This is known as training the mother.

3. Turning on the faucet is supposed to help a child get the idea of what is expected of him. For years our water bill was higher than our grocery bill.

4. It is wise to have a child's toilet seat in both the upstairs and downstairs bathrooms. I call this the "two-potty system."

5. Be neat and don't leave diapers lying on the bed. Put them in a pail. I had one kid who had a diaper rash on his face!

6. Do not try to budget your diapers. It's amazing how a baby can get so wet on only 4 ounces of milk.

Potty training is supposed to be done in a month's

time, but it is always held over. A child is "half trained" for years. During this time, you'll be wise not to take him into anybody's house, much less let him sit on anybody's lap. Attend only outdoor af-

fairs such as picnics and Cherry Festivals. I knew one kid who emptied a Tea Room during the peak business hour.

But be optimistic. You *can* get school lunch buckets that will hold two dry diapers.

Actually, I don't know what's so hard about toilet training. Every time they'd wet—I would go to the bathroom and cry.

2.
MEET MRS.
DR. FRANKENSTEIN

A Day In The Life Of A Two

I thought it might be a good idea to give some typical highlights in the day of an average two-year old, so you don't feel there is anything unique in your suffering.

At 5:00 a.m. the two-year old wakes up and runs into the parents' bedroom. He can't believe the ugly woman in bed is the same one that put him to bed last night.

Mother puts the kid back in bed. Kid stays there 5 minutes and finds time drags so he goes back to parents.

Kid climbs into their bed. Mother screams at kid to get off electric blanket with wet diaper.

Mother half asleep changes kid. Kid gets pricked with diaper pin and howls. Mother wakes up more. Mother puts kid back into his bed.

Kid climbs back into bed between parents. Mother tells father to put kid back into his bed. Father is snoring. Kid gets deferment. Kid doesn't lie still one second. He kicks mother in hip so hard she wonders if it's fractured. Mother gets up.

Kid watches mother open drapes and look at rain. He listens to mother say, "Damn it."

Mother struggles hard to get vitamins down kid, but can't. It's just as well since the vitamins are giving kid the pep to fight her off.

Mother gives kid orange juice, telling him it will make him a big man. Kid is evidently happy being a little kid because he spills orange juice.

While mother is brushing her teeth, kid squeezes out entire contents of tooth paste tube. Kid gets spanking. Mother hurts hand. Next time will use hairbrush.

Kid goes to toy box and gets tinker toys. He spills them all over living room floor and walks away. Mother tells him three times to pick them up and he says, "No!" each time. Mother steps on one, turns her ankle, and picks them up herself.

Kid tips over lamp. Only bulb breaks because all lamps in house are now unbreakable. He looks around for mother to come and give bawling out. She arrives and starts lecture. Kid's chin quivers, and he puts out his arms to be picked up. This is an act that has caught on, and works again.

Mother comes into living room and notices contents of ash tray all over carpet. A two-year-old is not innocent until proven guilty—she looks him up and bawls him out.

Mother goes to bookcase and gets Dr. Spock.

Kid sits down one minute. He starts to "think sink." Goes into bathroom, runs water and splashes it all over walls and floor. It is obvious the two-year old has done more than any other group to popularize the paper towel.

Mother tells kid they're going to have to have an understanding. They don't.

Mother goes to mirror and checks for gray hairs. Finds two and blames kid.

Kid decides to investigate buffet drawer. He gets chair and climbs up on it. Pulls drawer out too far and it falls upside down on the floor. Kid gets bad scolding. Kid wonders why mothers can't remember two-year-olds are people.

Kid gets mother's lipstick and applies it profusely to face and everything in sight.

Grandma stops by in the nick of time, and tells mother she is too strict. Kid goes into his room to play. In five minutes Grandma gets up to check and see if kid's all right. Mother physically stops Grandma from checking by tackling her around the legs. Grandma leaves.

Kid wants candy right before lunch and mother refuses. Kid lays on floor and kicks. Tantrum gains momentum and mother gives in.

Mother goes to bookcase and gets *Between Parent and Child*.

Mother puts good balanced lunch in front of kid on high chair tray. He picks at it a few minutes and then falls asleep into it. Mother goes to dictionary, checks symptoms of "rickets."

Mother carries kid to bed for afternoon nap. Kid wakes up as mother is tiptoeing out of bedroom. End of afternoon nap.

Mother asks kid if he has to go potty. Kid feels it's none of her business and says, "No." Kid goes a minute later.

Kid climbs up on chair and starts washing dishes. He gets spanking because he has dripped water all over floor from dish cloth.

Kid runs out when meter reader comes in. He comes back in soaked, and tracks mud on newly waxed kitchen floor.

Mother gives kid graham cracker. He walks into bathroom and dips it in toilet bowl. Then he goes into the living room and proceeds to press soggy mess into davenport. At first it goes on the dark flowers in the print and doesn't show. Kid realizes his mistake and concentrates on white part.

Kid then goes into bedroom and tries to restyle mother's wig. Mother discovers him at this activity too late and says some words that would have been bleeped out on television. Kid realizes apologies won't help so goes on to something else.

Mother goes to bookcase and gets book on mental health.

Mother gives kid 25 suggestions of what to do, and kid doesn't like any of them.

Mother calls office and asks to speak to husband. When husband gets on phone, mother sobs hysterically. Only words understandable are, "I can't stand it." Father offers to take mother out for the evening. Mother hangs up and calls 10 babysitters before she finally gets a jockey on the off season. Tells him to bring his whip.

Mother hunts for soap flakes until she remembers kid spilled the whole box yesterday.

Mother phones a friend and talks about kid the whole time.

Kid turns somersaults, hoping mother will hang up and watch him. Kid soon realizes why vaudeville died.

Kid pulls everything out of bottom cupboards. Tears labels off cans. Mother tears her hair.

Father comes home to harassed looking mother. Kid is playing with big scissors. Father objects. Mother assures father that in the morning they had looked dangerous to her too.

Every day is different, but worse.

3.
"RAIN, RAIN GO AWAY"
AND OTHER SONGS
MY CHILDREN TAUGHT ME

May I Borrow A Cup Of Tranquilizers

From three to five are the most nerve-wracking years. You must face the fact that there is nothing between the playpen and school, and just because your child showed the "terrible two" symptoms at one, it doesn't mean he's a genius. At this age children wear out parents faster than they do shoes. They seem to delight in causing mothers nervous breakdowns. I know one kid who was so bent on this, he took nursery school by correspondence! It's not always possible to stay a safe distance from your children. You may find that the only way you can get away from your kid is by barricading yourself in your bathroom or hiding behind the davenport.

If spending the day in the john becomes tedious, when leaving the arena remember the following principles:

1. The most important part of child care is safety. Learn to protect yourself!

2. Don't let them lift weights if you don't.

3. Drinking helps sometimes — if you give them enough.

4. There is one advantage of having pre-school children. Summer vacations aren't upsetting.

Mothers generally agree that it's worth suffering 364 days a year to have your children around you at Christmas.

I Never Met A Baby-Sitter I Didn't Like

I am sure there is no mother this side of a mental institution that refuses to treat her children to a baby-sitter. Whenever possible I would leave the kids and get out. My present baby-sitter has money in a Swiss bank, and our last one holds a second mortgage on the house.

Once the sitters tried to up their prices, but I was firm. Three dollars an hour and they supply their own ammunition.

Baby-sitters are getting so independent now. We have one in our neighborhood who only sits for couples who don't have any children.

1. If you want to keep a sitter, tell your kids to yawn as soon as the sitter arrives. This encouragement

will help make sure she stays until you've gotten
away.

2. Have some of your children out visiting when she
   gets there, and return home after you've left. She
   may not stay if she is greeted by them en masse.

3. Instead of simply refusing to tell the baby-sitter
   where you can be reached, it looks better to say,
   "We haven't decided yet where we're going."

4. The last time I had a baby-sitter, I called to ask how they were doing. One of the kids answered, "She can't come to the phone right now — she's cooking." A neighbor saw the smoke and untied her just in time.

5. I know one mother who when she is about to leave a party says, "I'll have one for listening to the baby-sitter's report."

6. Since the Horror Movie craze I haven't had too much trouble getting sitters—it's like getting paid $2\frac{1}{4}$ double features. One 18 year old turned white overnight. Now they just turn the TV off and watch the violence among the kids.

7. I offered one a magazine to read and she said, "No thanks, I'd rather just poke through the drawers."

8. I should have suspected this girl when I asked her to come over. She said, "Sure, what's the address of your kitchen?"

9. This girl had such an appetite, the first thing we did when we got home was go upstairs and count the kids.

10. We finally figured out a way to make sure our baby-sitter watched the baby. We put it in the refrigerator.

11. Our last agency dropped us ... Mother Kelly's Commandos. Now the Peace Corps is the last possible place we can find one.

12. None of my kids cried when we left the house, but we often had baby-sitters that did.

To save on baby-sitters — take your kids to an orphanage and tell them to mingle!

The Really, Truly "Happy Hour"

Raising a family means you always have something to look forward to—bedtime! But, unless you can pull them up by wires hooked to their clothing, like in Peter Pan, you're going to have a few problems when you say, "Run upstairs to bed."

Here are a few suggestions that may be helpful:

1. Make the first request at least three hours before you want them to go.

2. Try to develop timing so you can get them off during the split second between the commercial and the beginning of the next program.

3. Start putting disinfectant on their cuts.

4. Let them fall asleep on the floor — and then get them into their pajamas. You might get some helpful tips on how to do this from a local undertaker.

5. Hold off teaching them how to tell time as long as possible. In this way, you can point at 6 o'clock and say, "See, it's 7 o'clock, time for bed."

6. Sic the dog on them!

7. Dope their dessert!

8. Tell them it's Christmas Eve.

At this point I might say that I've always considered the real danger of smoking to be the chance of waking the kids when I go upstairs to get my cigarettes.

Out Of Bed—Down The Stairs—Into Your Heart

When your child gets out of bed don't let him stay up. Tell your kid that you owe it to the TV star that

fought so hard for prime time to give him your full attention.

But getting your child back into bed is a problem. The average parent is not a hypnotist. A dab of Elmer's glue on the back of his pajamas won't work, and it doesn't help to present a petition to your child signed by you and your husband.

Kids always have wonderful reasons for their being up instead of down:

1. He heard a noise and he came down to defend you.

2. He wants to put fresh water in your denture cup.

3. Two pages of his Dr. Seuss book are stuck together with jelly and he needs a razor blade.

4. He needs a black pencil to draw a mustache on Cinderella.

5. He just thought of an item to be added to his Christmas list that will make it an even 500.

6. There is a dragon in the attic breathing fire.

7. He just remembered he forgot to feed his turtle.

8. There is something alive in the closet and it is growling.

9. He's thirsty.

10. He forgot to kiss you goodnight.

I cured my kids of that "I want a drink" bit in a hurry. I hooked up a hose to the crib post.

Start Out By Banking On A Spanking

I believe in discipline. In fact, I believe in violence.

Try to remember what you say to your kid when scolding. Once I was giving a bawling out to one and another one spoke up and said, "Hey! That's my lecture." Scolding is rarely adequate. There are times when corporal punishment is necessary.

Make The Punishment Fit The Crime

If he . . .	*You . . .*
1. Shaves the cat	1. Make him wear a Tiny Tim wig to school
2. Trades his bicycle for a baseball card collection	2. Get him a paper route
3. Lets the tub overflow	3. Make him stay in the tub for a couple of days

When you pick punishments be careful to pick ones that they will hate but won't be too hard on you.

Strait jackets *are* not approved for children, even if they are appliqued with Mother Goose figures.

Learn From The Master—Threaten

Different threats work for different mothers. One I get results with is, "Clean up your plate or you have to eat dessert."

No wonder kids today are not so good. Old fashioned methods of discipline have been taken away from us. You can't drag your kid out to the woodshed and hit him with an electric razor. Hair brushes are plastic and break at the first blow.

Your kid won't be phased by your threatening to cut his allowance if you aren't giving him one.

1. Tell him he'll have to sit in the corner until his M & M's melt in his hand.

2. Threaten to make him sweep up the sand at Nursery School to pay his tuition.

3. Tell him if he doesn't behave, you'll let Grandpa fish for his guppies.

4. Tell him you're going to take him to the doctor's for a "Be Nice" shot to be administered with a big, blunt, rusty needle.

5. Instead of marshmallows, threaten to put cotton balls in his cocoa.

6. Tell him you're going to spend his birthday present money to pay for tint to cover the grey hairs he's giving you.

7. Let him know that if he gets dirty again you'll

wash his clothes while they're still on him. This threat is more effective if you have a wringer-type machine.

Be definite. Don't ask questions. Most parents goof up verbal chastisements. What sounds more ridiculous than asking a child, "Do you want a spanking?"

After all, you can always tell him that if he doesn't behave *you* are going to run away.

Promise Him Anything

If you can't get your way with violence and threats, sometimes a simple bribe will work wonders.

Bribes are used in politics, and parents who are as desperate as politicians should certainly feel free to use this method in child raising.

1. Promise to air condition his sand box.
2. Guarantee you'll get him on the Ed Sullivan Show to do his somersaults if he promises not to do them in the living room.
3. Tell him next time he makes mud pies you'll let him squirt real whipped cream on them.
4. Promise he can invite all his friends to the funeral of the next pet that dies and that he can have a five-car funeral procession.
5. Tell him you'll buy him all the things advertised on the commercials before, after and in the middle of every TV program he watches quietly.
6. He can have his own car when he's 10.
7. He can keep his horse in his bedroom.
8. He can live on Tootsie Rolls for one solid year.
9. He never again has to go to the dentist.
10. He can spit on the girl next door.

What To Do When The Screaming Starts
Or
A Mother's Guide To Non-Medical First Aid

When they are hurt and start screaming, remain calm. It is wise to find out where they are injured and examine the wound. Once I got so excited I put disinfectant on top of Ketchup. Another time I called the doctor when a kid woke up crying he couldn't lift his head off the pillow. A specialist discovered he was stuck to it with bubble gum that fell out of his mouth while he was sleeping! But when your kid gets hurt and comes home, you can't say, "I don't want to get involved."

1. Don't let your child stay home everytime he complains he is sick. Why do you think they have ambulances? To take a kid to school, regardless.

2. Elmer's Glue or Scotch Tape can fix most things that children break, except arms and legs.

3. If at all possible, wait until at least two of the kids are sick before you can call the doctor so you can get a package deal!

4. If their resistance is really down—attack.

Many schools ask you to fill out a form giving an alternate mother to call in case you aren't home when your child has an emergency at school. It isn't fair to write "Notify her first" after her name.

Cain And Abel

I don't like to say our kids fought a lot, but I always referred to our pediatrician as "Medic." In fact, the main advantage of having an only child is that one can't fight!

Get a pet for your children. It teaches them to love something. This is much easier than teaching them to love each other.

1. Usually, girls object to living under the same roof with their sister. In fact, she usually objects to living under the same sky! The only things they want to share are each other's clothing.

2. Try to have your daughters use separate rooms. With only a room divider, there are too many "border incidents."

3. Even if it is hard to dust, the only satisfactory room divider between two sisters is barbed wire.

4. Many people use misleading phrases like brotherly love. Cats and dogs get along much better than brothers.

5. Have your kids keep track of the number of fights they had while you were out so you'll know how good a time you had.

There is never any certain way to find out how the fight really started unless it happened in a bank where they have photographic equipment.

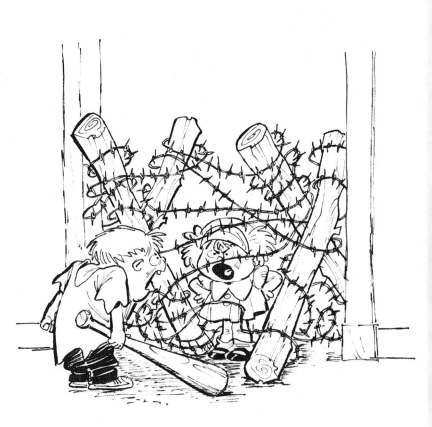

But Referee Harry Goldstein Gets Paid

Only adults say, "I'll meet you outside in the alley." You have to live with the fact that children's fighting is usually done in the middle of the room or at the table. Fights are continuous because all kids are completely selfish. The only thing they share willingly is chicken pox or mumps!

The other day one of my kids said: "Can I have a nickel for ammunition?" They can't agree on anything—we had a dog with five different names. He finally had a nervous breakdown – the two names that really mixed him up were Hildegarde and Robert.

There is nothing new under the sun that kids have not fought about. The following were the causes in some actual case histories of kids' fights.

1. A little girl claimed her brother's vitamin pill was a brighter shade of red.

2. A bloody battle ensued when a boy colored one ear in his sister's 250-page Mickey Mouse coloring book.

3. A girl found out by counting that her sister had one more blueberry in her piece of blueberry pie.

4. A kid took the bunk bed ladder to make a tree house while his brother was still sleeping on the top berth.

5. A boy made a sling shot with his sister's garter belt.

When they start fighting I just hand out candy. They have their choice of three flavors ... equinal, seconal, or morphine.

Actually I hate to stop it. It's the only thing they do together.

All those battles and a mother isn't even entitled to have a flag draped over her casket!

Wetting His Security Blanket

If a child takes off all his clothes and stands nude in the center of the dining room table, you can be pretty sure that child needs more attention. But that's the exception. In fact, kids today are too secure. To counteract this evil, here are a few suggestions.

1. When you go on a trip tell him you're putting his tricycle in the car so if you let him out along the way he won't have to walk home.

2. Take apart his bed, lay it beside the things you're planning to give to Goodwill.

3. In with the sack lunch he brings to Nursery School put his pajamas and toothbrush with a goodbye note.

4. When out shopping, put him into the window at the pet shop with a price tag that says: MARKED DOWN.

5. Tie a couple of bed sheets to the bed and drop them out the window. Then make a path of candy to the window.

6. At the Supermarket, put him in someone else's grocery cart.

7. Tell him, "You'll go far in life because you're the type people remember, Harry . . . I mean, Phillip."

The Malady Lingers On

Relatively new mothers often face the dilemma of deciding whether or not it is really necessary to call the doctor. So you'll know what is cause for concern, here are a few signs to look for:

If your child goes to bed around the fifth time you ask him to.

If he *walks* to the window when a siren goes by.

If he doesn't beg for what the commercial is advertising.

If there is a ball lying on the floor and he doesn't throw it.

If he lets you watch the Today Show instead of Captain Kangaroo.

If he wears the clothes you laid out for him.

If you've said, "Stop that darn fighting" less than ten times that day.

If you clean out his toy box and he watches silently while you discard the broken ones.

However, do not report these symptoms when you make the phone call to the pediatrician. What do they know about children? They're in an office all day long!

His Middle Name Is Benedict Arnold

When you have children it's not always possible to make a good impression—in fact, almost never.

A guest in your home invariably brings out the anecdotal conversationalist in your child. They find wonderful things to talk about:

1. The many times they were allowed to skip their baths.

2. How frequently you let them sip alcoholic beverages.

3. The black sheep of your family and their escapades.

4. The way you cheat on your income tax.

5. How you once made a hole in one and wrote down "zero."

If they become obnoxious showing off in front of company, make them chip in on the refreshments. If you can't think of anything to say, here are some sample statements you might use:

1. And I suppose you'd call out the National Guard for one kid?

2. I'm going to get help. Just today I mailed a post card to Rotten Kids, P.O. Box 230, New York, New York.

3. I'd stop him, but he's really not doing those things now. This was filmed earlier.

4. He's keeping our marriage together. Neither of us wants custody.

5. It helps us with our other kids. We use him as a bad example.

6. I'm just taking care of a neighbor's kid.

7. We'd return him but we don't know where he came from.

The Idiots And The Box

The two first letters my kids learned were TV. They watched so much they used to hop around the house because they thought Bugs Bunny was their mommy.

Here are a few helpful suggestions regarding television. Remember, it is easier to turn television sets louder than it is to turn kids lower.

1. Try to locate a TV set that only gets one channel. This will eliminate hundreds of thousands of fights.

2. If you don't feel like turning off TV while your kids are doing homework, you can ease your conscience by telling yourself you're preparing them for living in a college dormitory.

3. On rainy days mothers are not obligated in conscience to censor their children's TV viewing. Violence on TV might prevent violence in the home.

4. Learn how to handle your children. If cartoons are pre-empted by a news special say something like, "You just sit there and keep watching. Soon Batman will fly in and rescue the head of the Urban League."

If This Isn't Love

Trying to read, "I love you, Mommy," into their actions takes a lot of skill, but this art can be developed. Here are a few examples:

1. He throws food on the wall—so you can test your new detergent.

2. He makes you scream and shout—to develop your lung power.

3. He puts toys in every corner of every room — to help you keep your waistline.

4. He gets holes in the knees of pants and soles of shoes within one week—so you can claim his $600 deduction with a clear conscience.

5. He prevents you from reading a complete paragraph without interruption — so you'll never develop eye strain.

6. He leaves roller skates on steps — so you get acquainted with an orthopedist.

7. He says, "Shut up!" — so you'll rest your vocal cords.

Is One Too Young For Nursery School?

A mother who says she is sad to see her child go off to school will lie about other things. She will probably tell you she enjoys ironing and loves to go to the school for parent-teacher conferences regarding her children's behavior. She will tell you she feeds a family of six on $35.00 a week. This woman is a troublemaker. Avoid her.

My experience leads to the conclusion that kindergarten enrollment blanks should come gift wrapped.

1. I sent my kid to kindergarten with mixed emotions — joy mixed with ecstasy mixed with relief mixed with. . . .

2. Try to control your emotions when your children leave the house the first day of school. Once I turned a cartwheel and broke my ankle.

3. When he came home I asked him what he did all day, and he said the teacher asked him to cut some things out. I asked him what they were and he said, "Smoking and swearing."

4. Actually the kid was in a panic. The teacher said everyone must learn to spell his first name and he didn't know if his began with a 2 or a 5.

5. My neighbor told me, "Look at it this way, you're not losing a daughter — the teacher is gaining a migraine."

4.
MOMMY IS
THE ROOT OF ALL EVIL

The Impossible Years

You don't always have to wait until your children are teenagers to tell you they are going to turn out all right. Here are a few signs to watch for so you'll know your offspring is something less than perfect.

1. If someone calls and says, "May I please speak to Ronald's handler?"

2. If when your child skips school, the teacher doesn't report him to the truant officer.

3. If the neighbors chip in and pay for your liability insurance.

4. If the teacher sends an application blank home for your child to become a foreign exchange student, and he's the only one in the sixth grade that got one.

5. If when you look out your front window you can see more than five "For Sale" signs.

6. If your kid attends school in a mobile classroom and it pulls out some night.

7. If your child has had a tandem bicycle over a year and the second seat has never been used.

8. If the child's grandmother says, "I won't come over until he's asleep and tied down."

It Was My Kid's Birthday Party But I Was The One Who Aged

My daughter just turned six. And she wanted to have a birthday party. But I made two mistakes. The first was saying yes, and the second mistake was letting her turn six. Six is a very difficult age.

You're too old for Art Linkletter and too young for Dear Abby.

We had a problem. Some of the mothers didn't want their children to come just because we had a little accident at my last party. Four kids almost drowned while ducking for apples.

I decided to let her have the party; after all what could happen at a birthday party for a group of 6 year olds—that my insurance wouldn't cover.

Finally the great day dawned. I watched the kids come up the walk. They looked so neat and well mannered. I tried to make them feel at ease. I told them, "Just make yourselves at home" and they did. One boy ruined the sofa.

One kid kept picking his ear through the whole party. I found out later, his Japanese radio fell in.

I sent out 14 invitations and 76 kids came. I sliced the cake so thin, when one kid bit into it, he cut his mouth.

Kids love to show off in front of their friends. I once made the mistake of giving my kid an opening when I said, "You blew out all the candles – now, what's your birthday wish?" – he replied, "That I won't have to eat a piece of your cake!"

Due to the City Ordinances, I decide to have the celebration outdoors and off the ground. Since I couldn't afford to rent a plane—we had it in a tree.

After I got the kids up there, I took the ladder away.

I said to them, "It's too nice a day to stay in the house. A little lightning isn't going to hurt you."

I thought I was doing pretty good as the hostess. Then I heard one boy say, "If she was my mother, I would run away from home."

What shocked me most was when I came in and discovered a six year old kid was smoking—an eight year old had set fire to him.

Kids always reflect the habits of their parents. Some of them bragged, some were loud—some were quiet—and one boy spiked the punch. I didn't notice anything unusual until a little boy staggered up to me and said, "What's a nice girl like you doing in a place like this?"

I was desperate. There was only one thing left to do. So I put a sign out front—"Adoption Agency." I got rid of every one of those kids in less than an hour, including two of my own, and that night I got calls from every one of the parents thanking me.

After they left, our bird had a nervous breakdown.

Party Rules Amy Vanderbilt Never Knew
Or
Are Your Parents Picking You Up, Or Your Parole Officer?

Birthday parties make you realize the luckiest people in the world are those with children born on February 29. There are some tricks of the trade which I can pass along:

1. Make it a Bring Your Own Furniture Party—and store yours.

2. Leave the windows open during the party. There's a good chance a neighbor may break it up by calling the police.

3. Have a prize for the kid that first says, "I want to go home."

4. Try calling the living room the recreation room and vice versa. Children never play in the room designated for play!

5. Try a crooked game of hide and go seek. See if you can get them to hide in a room that locks from the outside.

6. Learn how to slip a "mickey" in the Koolade.

Get Him Something You'll Enjoy

I gave my youngest kid an unbreakable toy. So what happened, he broke all his other toys with it.

Toys nowadays are so realistic. I bought my son a toy dog that walks and barks. Every time we pass a tree, its batteries fall out. There are some presents, however, which are more fun to give than to get:

1. An apartment of his own on the other side of town.

2. A shark for his plastic swimming pool.

3. A space-suit with a self-destruct mechanism.

4. A magic kit where you can really make him disappear.

5. An electric train with 60 miles of straight track.

6. A shirt with a high collar that buttons over the mouth.

7. A Superman Suit that really makes it possible for the kid to fly off into space.

8. Then you can always try a child guidance toy.... We gave one to the neighbor's kid. It was a map.

I once bought one of my kids a hammer for his birthday, but I had to take it back. It didn't come with instructions.

It's amazing what kids can do without once they get them.

Gas Stations I Have Known

Anybody who calls an automobile a pleasure car has never ridden with my kids. There's just nothing quite like a family car trip—thank goodness!

I thought the movie "War Wagon" with John Wayne was about a couple taking a ride with their kids in their station wagon.

I have to stop at the garage every thousand miles and have my ulcers relined.

Always keep in mind Mother Diller's hard won travel tips.

1. Drive around in your own neighborhood for several hours until they've remembered everything they forgot to bring.

2. When you get a traffic ticket with your kids in the car, ask him to make out a few more. They're apt to whine all the way home if they don't get one!

3. While traveling always keep something in your purse to surprise them with—like a black-jack.

4. Be prepared for plenty of comfort stops. I've been driving for 27 years and I've never been in the left lane.

5. If, when you look in the rear view mirror, it's like watching a bullfight in a breadbox, there is a way to solve the problem. Put them in the trunk.

We take our kids everywhere but they still manage to get back.

Sorry We Have To Spill And Run

Before taking your kids out to eat, teach them some manners. Many restaurants have a misleading sign that says "We serve family style," but this does not mean spilling milk or throwing mashed potatoes.

1. Eat at a restaurant where reservations are not necessary. Once they have your name you can be billed for damages.

2. Eat early. Other patrons will be still having cocktails which will help them put up with you.

3. Don't worry about the amount you tip. No matter how much it is, the waitress will think she didn't get enough for what she had to go through.

4. Don't scold your kid when he spills, or he'll really start acting up. Say something like, "What poorly coordinated soup."

5. You might as well order a child's portion too, as that's all you'll get time to eat.

However, it is best to forget about eating out with kids. As soon as they get old enough to behave in a restaurant, they start ordering steaks!

A Child's Garden Of Vices

Get a perfect family home. That means one so ugly that you enjoy watching the kids tear it apart.

1. Don't think your kids are going to be less destructive just because they have a lot of things to entertain them. We got our kids a swimming pool and they capsized the house.

2. When you have kids, have you noticed how the grass always looks greener on the other side of the fence? That's because when you have kids, you don't have grass.

3. If your kids crack the plaster, paint it and put a frame around it. It will look like a mosaic.

4. Too many kids think of their home as one big coloring book. When I tell you I have lined drapes, I mean my drapes have crayon lines drawn all over them.

There'll Be Friction If It's Fiction

Don't worry if your child occasionally tells a fib. In this way he'll enter adulthood with experience. A little girl tattletale grows into a woman who is asked

to join countless bridge clubs and a little boy liar can grow up to be a politician.

Here are a few tell-tale signs to watch for so you'll know whether or not your child is lying.

1. If he has an alibi written out and reads it to you.
2. If he says, "If I'm lying, may I drop dead!" and adds, "Kevin can have my erector set."
3. If he says, "I didn't hit him until he hit me back."
4. If he says it followed him home and he is dragging it on a 2 inch thick rope.
5. If he says the teacher kept him after school and there is seaweed hanging on his jacket.

Sex Education Belongs In The Home

A few years ago some childless expert decided that the only answer to a child's question, "Where did I come from?" is the truth. The reason this happened was because he couldn't think of any modern evasions that would convince today's child. Do not tell your child the stork brought him. I was told this as a child and I believed it until I was 21. Perhaps this was because I looked so much like a stork! For six years I kept my kids innocent with the following answers:

1. You were tucked inside a box of soap flakes.

2. The Welcome Wagon Lady gave you to us the day we moved in.

3. You were the bonus gift I got for giving a Tupperware party.

4. I got you with green stamps.

5. You were left on my doorstep by fairies.

6. I had the exterminator in one day and when we left, the bugs were gone, but you were there.

7. I was working in the rock garden one day and I picked up a huge rock, and you were under it.

Teaching your kids the facts of life is a tremendous responsibility. I like to approach it gradually. I use artificial flowers.

1. Try not to act embarrassed. Don't explain things with your back to the child, and keep your eyes open.

2. Authorities suggest books to give children, but unless the required information is presented through Mad Magazine or Dell Comics, he won't read it.

3. I tried to explain the facts of life to my kids. I guess I didn't make things too clear because now they call me Daddy.

4. Fang explained the facts of life to the kids one day and when it was all over I asked one of the boys what he wants to be when he grows up. He said: "Either a bird or a bee."

5. My kids think a children's shop is a place where they sell kids.

After they stop asking where they came from, they start telling you where to go.

The Man From F.L.U.N.C.L.E.

At our home the day my kids get their report cards is known as D-Day.

Some parents console themselves when their

children get low marks by thinking they're too honest to copy from others. Don't make this mistake. It may just be that they are just too stupid to know who's smart and who's dumb and copy from the wrong person.

I won't say he cheats on tests. Let's say he always tries to sit behind round-shouldered honor students.

My kids are so dumb. One stayed up all night studying the toothpaste test.

I don't think my kid is very good in history. Yesterday I asked him, "Who was Columbus?" He answered, "He was the gem of the ocean," and he thinks that Alexander Graham Bell invented the graham cracker.

I asked my kid if he was learning anything and he showed me his Biology notebook . . . the July issue of Playboy.

When the arithmetic teacher asked, "If you reached in one pocket and pulled out 20 cents and you reached in another pocket and pulled out 80 cents—what would you have?" He answered, "Somebody else's pants."

Last night my oldest kid came home from school with a big gold star. A policeman was wearing it. He claims that he is an honor student . . . "Yes, Your Honor; No, Your Honor."

He Never Does That At Home

I've got a feeling my kid is causing trouble in school. Yesterday, he brought home a note asking for a written excuse for his presence. But I don't understand it. After all, how much trouble can you get into standing the corner.

Then I got a letter from the school telling me one of the kids is flunking. I don't know why they bother me. I'm not teaching them.

Finally I got an invitation to a teacher conference. Well, it wasn't exactly an invitation, it was a subpoena. I'm getting one complaint after the other. Now I'm spending more time with their teachers than they are.

1. The teacher wanted to know if the kids spent too much time watching television. I had to admit they watch it constantly. And I'm a little concerned about it. Our set hasn't worked in two years.

2. He also wanted to know when the children did their homework. I said: "At dinnertime." He said: "While they're eating?" I said: "Instead of eating."

3. He asked me where my children study at night. I said, "In our car." He said, "Do you think that's a fit place for children to study?" I said, "Of course not. And I've often asked them to come in and join the party."

4. They said my kid didn't understand one thing about Algebra. Fang was indignant. He said: "That's impossible! We speak it at home."

When he left, I told Fang to help our son with his school work while he can. Next year the kid goes into the fourth grade.

Go And Tell

You can still look like the perfect parent and get rid of your kids by recommending they go on their school's overnight field trips to Washington, D.C., and if possible having them be a foreign exchange student.

Field trips provide you many hours of peace and quiet while you feel that at the same time your child is learning things he never could at home.

The following is a typical conversation between mother and child after such an educational adventure:

Mother: How did you enjoy the field trip?

Kid: It was fun on the bus.

Mother: What did you learn?

Kid: Other cars pull over farther when they see a bus coming.

Mother: Did Billie Burns go on the trip?

Kid: Yeah. He brought his frog.

Mother: How could he do that?

Kid: He had it in with his lunch and it got loose and went up the driver's pants leg and he went into the ditch and a truck had to come and pull the bus out and while they were doing that, we scared some cows and pretended we were hitch hiking. Jimmy Condon got picked up and nobody knows where he is.

Mother: Well, did you learn anything on the trip?

Kid: Karen Anderson carries a paper bag on the bus 'cuz she usually throws up.

Mother: I mean what did you learn inside the science museum?

Kid: You have to wait in line a long time before you get to go to the bathroom.

Let's Play Ring Around The Bath Tub

My son has a pen pal . . . it's a pig.

If there's one speck of dirt around for miles that kid of mine could find it—he gets dirty just getting out of the tub. We have the only home on the block with dirty soap.

Boys, in particular, will try to talk you out of baths. They seem to have the idea they're non-immersible.

1. Some dirty spots on arms and legs can be passed off as bruises. However, black and blue ears are a rarity, so you had better wash them.

2. To get the dirt off their elbows, try using coarse sandpaper.

3. When sending your son to the store, make sure he is clean above counter level!

4. Your kid doesn't bathe often enough if he thinks the towel racks are bookmarks for magazines.

5. Your kid is doing something wrong if, when he takes a bath, he leaves a ring around the room.

6. When our kids were young there were so many toys in the bath tub we bathed them in the toy chest. Finally we got to the point when bath time was a cinch. We lived around the corner from a car wash. We just put the kids in the car — and drove through.

I don't care what the kids do as long as they put papers down first.

Gin and Sympathy

Never give sympathy. Once you give it, every time a child comes in bleeding he will expect it. Instead, greet his plight with sarcasm!

1. He got caught in the rain and comes in soaking wet. Say, "I suppose *you* could make flowers grow by spitting on them."

2. He gets bitten while roughhousing with the puppy. Tell him, "You think he's like your father? — he can take his teeth out and put them in a cup while he plays with you."

3. Your little girl gets her finger pinched. "All that fuss over getting a finger pinched, and you expect to wear a girdle some day?"

4. His brother has hit him. Say, "Don't worry. I'll tell him he has to be out of town by sundown."

5. He gets punched in the nose by a playmate. Say, "From the fuss you're making, you'd think you were Jimmy Durante."

6. He is upset because somebody stole his tricycle. You say, "I'll take care of phoning the FBI, but you're going to have to pay for the call to Scotland Yard out of your piggy bank."

Don't Forget To Shut The Door

Most children threaten at times to run away from home. This is the only thing that keeps some parents going.

Do not make a commotion when this happens. The more casual the treatment of the affair, the less enthusiastic the fugitive becomes. Here are a few effective remarks to make when your kid is at the door with his suitcase.

1. Wait a minute until I give you your Social Security number in case we don't see you again before you're 65.

2. Go ahead and if a dog bites you remember you've already had tetanus shots.

3. Ditches are your best protection during a tornado.

4. Put more postage on your letters if they're sent from outside the country.

5. You can't leave until you've cleaned up your room.

Beware Of The Dog, The Cat, And The Fish

I was reading a Child Care and Baby Book the other day and ran across a chapter entitled: DO YOU REALLY KNOW YOUR CHILD'S FRIENDS? I certainly do: 4 snakes, 3 toads, a rabbit and a goldfish.

1. Be sure the dog you get as a pet for your kids doesn't bite. We got one that the owner assured us loved children—and he did. Better than hamburger or dog food.

2. Our dog was filthy. The kids never gave him a bath. Every six months we'd have him dry cleaned.

3. All children want to sleep with their pets. Mine had goldfish. It sure beats getting up in the middle of the night to get them a drink of water.

It's a sign your kid isn't happy if instead of having dogs follow him home, he follows dogs home.

Every Week My Kids Want Something I've Made Myself—Money

My kids know the value of a dollar. And that's why they have no respect for it. If I increase their allowance one more time, they move into a higher tax bracket. They use five dollar bills for bookmarks.

I know a man who had to file bankruptcy. He couldn't afford his kids' allowance.

Every parent should be prepared when his child asks for more money:

1. Remind him he is unskilled labor.

2. Tell him he won't be able to tell his kids how rough he had it if you raise it.

3. Tell him you'll have to think it over, and he might as well learn now that legislative machinery moves slowly.

4. Encourage his playing with younger kids. Their allowances are smaller.

Most men don't know which is cheaper: To stay married and give his kids an allowance or to get a divorce and pay alimony.

Want to know how to teach children the value of money? Borrow it from them. Pay it back within 24 hours unless you want to have a bill in the hands of a collection agency.

When they finally have it all, you can say, "Listen kid, do you realize you've saved up enough money to run away from home!"

Premature Senility

It's a good idea for kids to have idols, but watch who they are. My kids' fan club is for Rip Van Winkle. Kids are so lazy nowadays, they think elbow grease is a petroleum product.

1. Kids today say things like, "Should I brush my upper or lower teeth?"

2. Every so often a household product is advertised, "even a child can use it." Where did they ever find a kid that would use it so they could make the claim?

3. If you ask a kid to answer the door, he acts like you're breaking the child labor law.

4. One of our kids lay sprawled out in a living room chair so continuously that when he got sick we didn't know whether to call a doctor or an upholsterer.

5. This kid is really lazy. He wants to go steady but he can't find a girl that makes house calls.

6. No surgical team in the world can perform an ambition transplant. My next-door neighbor gave up. Now she is giving her eight year old Geritol!

7. We call Pete the ambitious one. "Ambitious" in our house means he's a light sleeper.

8. Finally I gave up. Now we just call the kids Winkin', Blinkin' and Nod.

The last thing any of them ever did for money was lose his baby teeth. I mean it's embarrassing when someone asks them the name of their last employer and they say, "The Good Fairy."

5.

LIFE

WITH

MOTHER

You Can't Mail Your Children Back To Dr. Spock

Jokes aside, my kids have never really been a problem. Of course, if they ever get out of the cellar....
We have it all fixed up so they can never get us into trouble. We've never told them their last name. I can summarize all I know about being a parent in five rules.

1. The only time to allow a child to run in the house is when he's on his way outside.

2. Don't always hide in the same place.

3. You should not have a favorite child, but if you do, if possible—have it one of the family!

4. Don't give all the gruesome details to childless couples. They're much happier thinking they missed something.

5. Never let your children get to the point where they ask the question: "What do you suppose my main trouble is . . . heredity or environment?"

But when you come right down to it I have an utterly fantastic relationship with my kids—I'm their mother.